WHEN THE SOUL SPEAKS

"BOOK OF DEEP POETIC STORIES"

WHEN THE SOUL SPEAKS

SPEAKS

"BOOK OF DEEP POETIC STORIES"

TAHARKA ANKHENATON

CITI OF
BOOKS

CITIOFBOOKS, INC.
3736 Eubank NE Suite A1
Albuquerque, NM 87111-3579
www.citiofbooks.com
Hotline: 1 (877) 389-2759
Fax: 1 (505) 930-7244

Ordering Information:
Quantity sales. Special discounts are available on quantity purchases by corporations, associations, and others. For details, contact the publisher at the address above.

Printed in the United States of America.

ISBN-13:	Paperback	979-8-90124-402-9
	eBook	979-8-90124-403-6
	Hardback	979-8-90124-404-3

TABLE OF CONTENTS

Dedication

This book is dedicated to my Mother, without my mother and Father I would not be here to share these stories. Regardless of my father's history, there's no me without parents. As you all are aware there's an Alpha-a beginning and an Omega-an end. If not for my mother, I would not exist. I pray she's blessed in the afterlife and is proud of what I was, what I am, and what I will always be. This book would have never been written with any of my spiritual intellect if not for my mother having me. Thanks, Mother of mine!

I would like to thank my soul mate Njeri Ankhenaton. As of this day of this dedication, my wife in short has endured the bitter and the sweet of being with me for over 3 decades. Life sometimes got so hard and unpredictable during life challenges that I told her to consider leaving me. But I remembered her staring me in the eyes and saying with conviction "I'm not going anywhere". She is the embodiment of her queen ancestors that stayed even at war and difficult times, changing bandages of warriors and giving them support until there was peace.

I dedicate this book to my diehard friends and family. So many family members I've taken from other families to make up my own. So many that can share in my success and so many that have passed on to the afterlife. Without you, I don't think I could have survived. Thanks to all my brothers and sisters for your time, talks, hugs, hospital visits, and those that were by my bedside praying I would make it. Well, here we are!

Acknowledgments

I would like to acknowledge all those who inspired me to keep writing and demanded that I one day write a book. There are so many of you from online forums, friends, associates, and complete strangers. Your responses were heartfelt and demanding for more. I truly appreciated the pressure and demands to write about certain life experiences that were personal but could inspire others.

I Against I

As a child,
I set alone in my room and feared the darkness,
The sounds when I closed my eyes echoed like steps, echoed whistling
and screeching noises,
I feared welts,

Welts of no imagination,
Welts of extension cords breaking my skin,
Welts of a paranoid schizophrenic father,
Welts of sin though sinless,
Welts of pain, can't say painless,

Beatings in the same spot made the area numb,
Thinking I was cursed by the Gods,
Father hates son,
Until they began healing,
Picking at the scabs, absent love feelings,
Back to the darkness, opening the closet,
Wondering what's that noise not being able to take it no more,
Though scared,
1 stepped into the closet and I saw I,

I against I,
No boogie man, demons or monsters,
It was I,
My fears, my tears created my own monsters throughout the years,
I really was all by myself,
Only I,
I against I,

So I go on, multiple shots, multiple scars,
Hood made bicycles before cars,
Thinking I grew beyond I, graduated,
Thoughts of military, work or college,
Evicted the day of high school commencement,
No more parent tutelage,
Mom made room for the family but not I,
So it's me against the world,
I against I,

My own decisions, my own benedictions, my own impressions, my
own reflections,
You don't know I so look deep within my eyes,
Tears fail to fall as my heart slowly calcify,
See the small child right before she was bitten by a black mamba in
South Africa,
Too late to save her,

As my partner attempts to reach out to her,
You could see life leave from her,
His eyes failed to see,
Slow-motionly,

She slowly stopped breathing,
Parents should have told her black mamba's burrow within hollow
trees,
There was nothing that could be done for thee,
Anti-venom too far away,
Listen and make this a lesson learned,

Warned but never taught,
Mother and father tears hold lifeless body scorned,
A city and village mourned,
Fighting the nightmares was I, I against I,

Nature is the coldest natural atrocity on planet earth, cold,
like child stillbirth,
Another story in America,
Distant land yet same outcome as South Africa,
Lying in the street,

A child shot lies, victim of ignorance,
Yet the child still dies,
This was shots fired from a black male not black mamba,
Your turf, my turf,

Lacking wisdom, culture & identity since birth,
In this low-life state,
Another lifeless child lye,
Unlike nature this is unnatural,
Living like it however we're not animals,

So many ruthless visions burned into my eyes,
Now eyes closed,
I against I.

A God!

I saw your fate & crushed it in my hands,
Many of you failed as my sons and daughters,
You failed as man,
Killing most of my creations your minds fail to understand,

I saw your pettiness & insecurities,
Like sewage in water impurities,
Despite my power of creating millions of different species,
You go on with less than spiritual activities,
Then claim hollow words of God bless you,
Or you're blessed by the best,
Oxymoronic of me knowing the evil in you,

Lost behavior's more important than me being the God in you,
I saw your hate plagued by the opinions of others,
Failing the God in them and their birthright creation of mothers,
Women of the earth who were made to be your equal,
Treating them like they're the sinful,
The decadence of man placed them below,
Knowing you cannot be born without them,

A weakness so pathetic & feeble,
Like a bone structure formed with no calcium,
No ancestral DNA in them,
So frail and in fear,
You destroy others not like you,
Though I created them just like I created you,
Though you ask for blessings,
Tell me what blessings you gave me?

And before you open your mouth to exhale the oxygen, I gave you to answer,
Know that you're not speaking to your peer group, empty friends or worldly masters,
You're answering the omnipresent constructor of the universe,
So, be careful telling me what blessings you gave me since birth?

And out of all your hate and differences,
Your anger was created to aid in your protection,
Not to be fooled by man's indifferences,
Man's frozen influences,
Nor your media masters behind the scenes foiled constitutional empty promises,
Words in print that's transparent pending which people it refers to,
Words that really shows a blank page removed by lost prophets of rage,
A singer lost for words that can't emit a sound to the microphone on stage,
Ancestors forgotten like you were their missing their wisdom and age,

When you prayed to me asking to repent,
The blessing was not allowed due to it only applying to the moment,
Like a fish that forgot it lives within the water around it,
So, when I don't answer you,
Instead of your repentance you question my existence,
Look at all this chaos you all allow saying a true & living God would not allow this,
You're reaping what you sow like failing to support a levee knowing a storm will hit,
Yet you fail me continuously like drug dependence,

Too weak to not use it in the 1st place,
Yet blame me instead of yourself when you lost God's faith,
Instead of looking in the mirror and blaming your face,

Whether you believe me to be afar or within you,
I've proven myself with everything you see without you,
Whether you fear me not answering you,
I answer you every time from within you,

Man has various depictions of me though not true,
Yet I am the science of man that allow your lungs to breathe,
I am the current in all your seas,
I am the wind and what stops at zero gravity in space,

I am the creation of the known & unknown in worlds you can't place,
There is nothing I have to do for you,
Since you were given eyes and fail to see,
Your duty is to live in the light of me,

I am the macrocosm of truth yet you decide your destiny,
And despite the little you know of science even with scientology,
You can't create a better me without the mind I gave that came from me,

In retrospect, you will never know a God and the power within me,
Only men who won wars try to tell you only being a small part of me,
Sons that often became my enemies like a parent killed by their own seed,
Plagued by physically destroying others in my name,
Yet none came before, and none will come after,
And despite you using the little you know about science to build,
You suppress saving others like a wall formed before you and yield,
Every time you open your eyes and look deep within them to see me,
Know that scientifically murdering and the ethnic cleansing others is
no representation of me!

Forgive Them Father, For They Know Not What They Do

I was raised hearing, "Forgive them father for they know not what they do",
Though my mother nurtured the strong, the weak and the misguided,
Do you recall someone not doing something intentionally to you?
If so,
You can forgive them,
Not the willful intent of the rest of them,
My mother I miss,
Studied 126 different religions and even they don't agree with the logic of this,
Open your mind to this,
Many planned to deceive you,
The 1st day they got the number from you,
Went out of their way to lie to you,
Fell off the path of righteousness and actually chose to go astray,
Refused spiritual plans to fall off the path to get blood on their hands,
They thought about it when getting dressed,
Loaded the gun with intentions to shoot in distress,
Had no plans to use their hands,
Eager to use a 3–12-pound trigger pull with one finger,
The unsettling fear to hear,
The sound barrier breaking in your ear,

You were told they loved you but done things like someone who hated you,
Forgive them father for they know not what they do?
Is a weak lie from the mentality of a slave under water told to behave,
That's deceived too weak to fight to breathe,

Use your arms and legs to push and stroke the water to the top,
And emerge like a submarine hitting the air to breathe,
Wipe the water from your eyes,
Open with the tunnel vision of a laser and see,
Although those that told you this loved you,
Your enemies know exactly what they do!
Those who caused harm to you know exactly what they do!
Those who would harm your children know exactly what they do!
Those who steal from you know exactly what they do!
Those who cheated and hurt your feelings looking you in your eyes
swearing it's not
true know exactly what they do!
Those who claim to be your friends, who know everything about you,
Used it against you talking behind your back know exactly what you do!
It's odd,
It's obvious they're not children of God,
Instead of forgiving them for a lie & untruth,
For believing this…you need to think what's wrong with you and who
taught this to you,

Why would you ask God, the most high, creator, grand architect of
the universe to
protect evil & forgive?
Instead ask that you're forgiven for what you do to those who
intentionally try to take
away your will to live!
You don't need a bible, koran, septuagint, torah, papyrus, dead sea
scrolls, 42 declarations of innocence or sad songs to rehearse,
To know that metaphysically self-preservation comes 1st!

They can be forgiven when they live to repent for their sins,
Not while they kill, threaten, lie, and deceive the future millennium &
our children,

When you cross over from your mental disease and become Children of God,
Then, and only then, can you be forgiven!

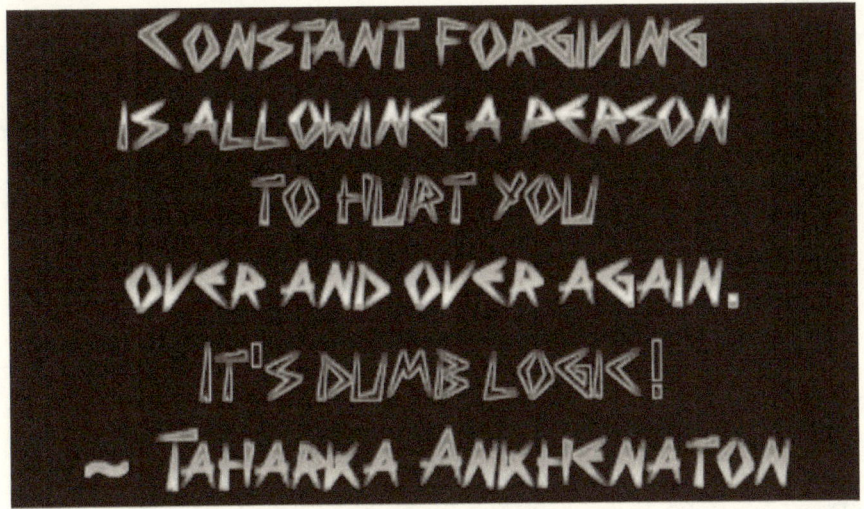

CONSTANT FORGIVING
IS ALLOWING A PERSON
TO HURT YOU
OVER AND OVER AGAIN.
IT'S DUMB LOGIC!
~ TAHARKA ANKHENATON

Cry Me A River

I'm not a God
Nor prophet
As an archangel
I'm not here to address your affairs
The Gods sent me to simply answer your prayers

Yet you're not forgiven
Your life is scarred and full of void
Continue on this path
So be your children

Be honest to yourself 1st
Then pray to the Gods to be
There's no hiding place
That the Gods can't see

Many go to church
A synagogue
A mosque
Fall to your knees alone
Prayed on the floor in the place they call home
Yet you continue to tell the Gods fables
Lie to yourself
Even when you blessed your food at your table
How would you answer why you act so superficial?
Why act so spiritual?
Why act like you care?
Constantly hurting others and having affairs
Not telling the truth
I have documented your countless lies as proof

How do you answer acting like you wanted to be one with God?
One day a week praying to be saved
Six days a week acting odd
Wanting angels as friends
Allowing your body to be abused by unholy men
Catching their untruths and holding a grudge
At one time they saw your beauty
Later they saw the sludge
For all you want to be forgiven for that differ
Cry me a river

Cry
Cry all your sins away
You would have to cry for days, months, years
Cry
Cry all your hatred of yourself away
Cry for all the times you gone astray
Cry for all the fallacies you told God were no more
Cry for every day you acted out the mentality of a prostitute or whore
Cry for the days you showed yourself with short skirts when sunny
Cry for when it was all about the money
Cry
Cry this river
Stand there and begin to cry this stream
Then and only then
Will you be free!
Reputable to be allowed into this kingdom
Free from your low-life stardom

You see
After you witness your fate
You will have to cry a river to be allowed into heavens gates
Praying to the Gods in sorrow will not do it
Make your words become actions

And do it
Until then
If ever
Cry me a river
Absent aid from the precipitation in the weather

Cry for ones that died due to lies like yours
Cry for the molested little boys and girls
Cry a river for all the rapes
Cry for all those that couldn't escape
The Antwon Fisher's
No where to go
They were innocent
Yet often you liked being low
Cry for all the civilians killed by war
Cry for the innocent
Cry for the lives taken by the tsunami's close to the shore

When you thought your life was all about you
Cry for the Malcolm's
The Martin's
World War 1 & 2
Cry for the deadly droughts
Cry for the starvation
Cry for the innocent still in incarceration
Cry for the curse
That it's apparent
Every generation not learning the history of the past
Is getting worse
Cry for all the tragedies you heard of before
Cry because you will not even be allowed to knock on heaven's door
Cry for what many call judgment day
Cry for what many call purgatory
Hell

The bottomless pit
Cry for you will not be alone
You will smell the scent
For the pit is not filled with fire and brimstone
How does one listen to this?
Hence the word bottomless

All this after your heart stops
You will see
Unless you cry a river for me
Since you lived your life with the demons and didn't differ
Cry
Cry me a river!
Written this 3rd day of August, 2006
By the author,
Taharka ankhenaton

Inspired by the record
"Cry me a river"
By Justin Timberlake

A Dream

She was lonely,
Aggravated with men,
Those who claimed they loved her,
Those that be-friend,
Despite how careful she was,
It happened over and over again,
For a moment it seemed like her heart died,
Thoughts of suicide,
Tired of adult boys,
She asked God for a man,
He fears led to tears,
Her mental tiredness made her weak,
Unclothed,
She fell asleep,
I came through her window,
Sharing her pain,
Blew warm air into her ears,
Gently used my tongue to ease her fears,
I can hear her low moan,
Yet faint,
In her whispers I heard "more",
I looked through the thin sheets,
I lightly licked and kissed her all over her body,
While lovingly doing this,
She moved in ecstasy,
I massaged and rub her,
Did everything but made love to her,
Told her that it's someone like me that would love you,
Speaking and licking around her ears,
Deep breaths but low blowing,

Took away all fears,
In her passion,
She didn't open her eyes,
Yet responding every time I touched her thighs,
So tired yet comfortably weak,
She fell asleep,
A gentlemen's candor I don't lack,
Softly put the thin sheets back,
I left a note,
Sounded like a quote,
"In this world"
"Someone loves you girl!"

A Fractured Spine

A King in a time men lack being men,
Is a sin to the kingship of mankind,
Like being born with 1/2 a mind,
Not born with sections of your spine,
Failing to walk a straight line,
The Goddess of the universe denying your kind,
Mother nature allowing you to be lost in the Bermuda Triangle,
Your low nature GPS and radar can't find,

You lack the testicular fortitude of the ancients blood flow,
The red, the black,
The green,
Your hemoglobin doesn't compare with mine,
As your genetics are off and your DNA fits that of a nerd,
Someone told you; you were a man though you lack leg strength to
follow the herd, Not
having the mental wherewithal to know who you are,
No wonder you follow spirits of drugs, money, hoes and cars,

You're like a tree that's hollow,
With no roots to fertilize the earth or follow,
The sad part of this truth,
Birds don't build nests instead they defecate on you,
You're like a killer bee kicked out the hive,
They sought through all that bs, lies and jive,
Since your mind is hollow allow me to remove your eyes,
The Gods turn their backs on you,
The Goddesses with hopes of you taking your throne, cries!
You had the ability to see yet didn't want to see,
That's why people like you are not like me!

The Gods must be merciful,
If left up to me,
Although blurred, I wouldn't allow you to see what I see,
Wouldn't allow you to breathe the air I breathe,
Wouldn't allow you to continuously make others bereave,
Deny your offspring's the ability to conceive,
Not only would you not look like me and my kind,
I would make your cranium hollow with brain fluid and no mind,
Since you don't belong on our throne,
Leave our spiritual women alone,
Repent acknowledging that you failed mankind,
In another life, bow down and hail to the throne,
Since you were never a part of us due to your spirit being sold,
Out into shark infested waters,
Alone!

A Prayer

God, I ask for help with all that aids me,
I ask for assistance with the harms of life,
I ask for your angels to protect me and my family,

Those close to me lord,
Those whom I would feel hurt if they're not here anymore,
Those in life that I may not see every day,
Yet I still feel for,

My God,
I ask to be embraced by your omnipresence wherever I go,
Forgive my limited geography,
For I know it's nowhere in this universe that you don't know,

In my life I will ask many things from you my lord,
The unknown is before me with multiple challenges for me to follow
through,
My lord,
What say you?

My child,
You ask many things from me,
What you ask is not considered much for me to do,
If you were a God who was often taken for granted,
What say you?

You ask for me when un-holiness and darkness surrounds you,
You ask for me when your so-called friends betray you,

You ask for me when all else fails,

You ask for me when you're beaten or miserable,
Manipulated, maimed or even sold for sale,

You decide right and wrong every day,
Yet you expect me to clean up your bad decisions when you pray,

When someone told you that I would forgive thee,
Did you think that you could do it over and over again?
Just pray to me and take me lightly?

You listen to others with twisted tongues that support your thoughts,
Yet you forget me like you don't have a voice,
Between right and wrong,
Truth is the choice,

It doesn't take a prophet to show you the right way,
I've blessed you with consciousness,
It was you who decided to go astray,
Yet my child,
You want me to protect you anyway,

Many times, you beseech me,
I remind you with obstacles and tests,
Yet often you feel comfortable forgetting all about me,

For all that are righteous and wholesome,
Why should I protect you so you may enter my kingdom?
You pray that I hear you,
Bless you,
Continue to think about you,
Instead of answering you,
I will think about what you want me to do for you,
Unconditionally,
You remember in your frail life,

Taharka Ankhenaton

Decisively begin to ponder,
What you are to do for me!

Am I Worthy, My Lord?

I've been to dark places,
Absent light,
The unholy prevails,
Absent these lands of love and kindness,
It's dark all the time,
When the sun comes out,
It's still dark,
I have walked through the valley of the shadow of death my lord yet I
feared evil,
Evil,
Evil that's so cold,
So confusing,
You never…really know evil,
When you think you have it figured out it changes form,
When you think you see its color like a chameleon,
I wish no such evil reaches these lands but I know it's here,
Thinking,
Contemplating,
Different shades and ways,
Different techniques,
Different speech,
You never really eliminate it,
You deal with it even if you have to become it,
A question for the judgment board,
Am I worthy my lord?

Is there a place for me around the holy?
I am feared yet I am tamed,
I am not crazy,
I am sane,

Maybe I will not be the one to teach the angels the right way,
Maybe I will not be the one to lead the group when we pray,
Instead of white I'll be happy to wear black,
At war...I will be there despite the stakes,
I'll even guard the gates,
A question for the judgment board,
Am I worthy my lord?

In the face of adversity when I am not wrong,
I stay strong,
Normally...I have few flaws,
In the face of evil,
Its manmade laws,
People can be so ignorant and unholy,
It seems as though they always end up around me,
They challenge me like I envision a demon challenging a saint,
A mistake,
I am embodied with another side that begins to make me hot all over,
I try to control it and back off,
But when they persist,
I explode like an enraged soldier,
Despite their size,
I'm not happy until I hear their cries,
Their pain,
Beat them sane,
Making them answer for what they've done to others,
Letting them know that angels too can mane,
For the right reason,
As if they committed treason,
Long-term wounds are a part of my life,
Several times I've been under the knife,
Losing is not an option but if I do that's fine,
Stronger I am the next time!
A question for the judgment board,

Am I worthy my lord?

Would you have a place for me?
Darkness has a way of blinding you,
And I often can't trust what I see,
What I feel or what I hear,
Spiritual people at the highest levels,
Was not sincere,
They told me to just pray,
Praying doesn't make people stop from going astray,
Falling into the abyss,
So-called spiritual followers that don't fight this,
Should be taken off your holy list,
I've seen the enemy's eyes,
The blues, the grey, the greens, the brown,
The sexy eyes like an aphrodisiac,
If I was to see clearly,
I should have seen all black,
All white,
Hatred and uptight,
Those whom want and crave the darkness instead of the light,
I do my best to stay away from them,
In every job I do,
Standing for righteousness,
I always find myself back around them,
When the wolves come,
Your children call on me lord,
Despite me trying to stay away from them,
I sometimes have to act no different than them,
In grey times,
One should learn that darkness is sometimes fought by a different
form of evil,
While some at night will have their worse fight,
In a different darkness,

Many will have a pleasant night,
Blackness surrounds you but you're not in fear,
You're comfortable as though you're supposed to be here,
You're embraced,
Not fearing any dark place,
In the lack of light,
Some share the night,
You see,
I'm called upon because that will be me,
Lastly,
Humbly speaking,
On bent knees,
Under these circumstances to the judgment board,
Am I worthy, my lord?

Clarity In Mental Masturbation

Just because I was bleeding from my wounds,
Tired, and my face bared a frown,
Don't mean I don't have enough energy to take out another one of
your big bozo clowns,

Whether you're in or out of town,
You need to learn the age old saying "don't kick a brother while he's
down",
I may be judged in time, only time will tell,

I realized a long time ago that I'm a candidate for God of War hell,
So I don't need your acceptance or friendship,
From no one that doesn't say what they think to my face, don't shoot
from the hip,
You laugh behind walls in minor to mankind groups,
People like me like to have people like you suck on soup,

My wounds have all about healed,
Skin and scar tissue is covered and no longer peel,
Bones are mending yet getting stronger,
Only a true warrior knows how this feels,

So, if you see evil in my eyes, I apparently don't know you,
It's for my own personal protection,
Not that I hate or don't like you, and if I do,
I apparently don't give a fuck about you!
My friends,
Love, live and die for me as I do for them,
We're not expendable,
In fact, we'll drop what we're doing at 3 in the morning,

Just to come get you on a whim,

Let me say,
In the darkness of my eyes
I am not evil yet it's evil within me,
It's evil in anyone who struggles and fights that wants to be free,
If you look for kindness,
I'll speak and be proper,
However, to really know if I'm kind you have to know me,
That's something you will not find in eye contact passing by,
If someone told you that's enough,
You're living a lie,

Many don't want to be burned when you've been burned before,
Many don't like getting jumped when you've been jumped before,
Many don't want to wake up after surgery again when they've been critically injured before,
Many don't like to be cheated on and tricked when others cheated and tricked you before,
As many don't give their hearts,
When others haven't shown you love before,

My friends love, fight, train, focus and be disciplined,
Because we like to be drama free,
Listen and learn from a warrior's wisdom,
Or choose to keep mentally masturbating, repeating history choosing not listen to me!

Difficulty Conceding

Hail to the throne I'm having difficulty conceding,
Why some people are actually breathing,
I was raised told by others black was a curse,
Then later found out to the world blacks gave them birth,
I was raised told we never created anything,
Then found out black man created air conditioning,
Boykin invented the 'electrical resistor' used in computers,
Radios and television sets,
As a black child looking at TV never knew to give him respect,
Every 57 days giving blood to the Red Cross,
Without Dr. Charles Richard drew creating the blood bank we would
have been lost,
I was lost, told this by people I adore,
Instead of breaking my mental slavery they actually were closing the door,
Their ignorance caused and insurmountable amount of confusion I
never felt before,
Awakened by my consciousness with brothers I tried to break bread,
Yet I was ousted, wondering was it something I said,
I never thought crabs liked being in a bucket,
Many people actually enjoy being stuck in it,
I realized many signed up to be drafted by the devil,
And many, would never be on my level,
Like war,
I actually respected it,
Like a God,
I never accepted it,
So, in my passion to actually learn more,
I awakened to another level of consciousness I never saw before,
My cultural class took me to a higher level of knowledge
Yet many, considered it sacrilege,

So I learned about the origin of religion and where it actually came from,
Only to find many saved people like being dumb,
It was like drugs was being given in a quest to be saved,
Not knowing it, sent right to their graves,
Eating foods that was forced on them as slaves,
So I went to program teaching culture, metaphysics, astrology and dietetics,
Actually, learning what you put in your body and what it does to it,
Even still, they never respected it,
It's like they actually opened their cranium, pulled out their brain and stomped it,
I watched drugs run rapid in my community,
In the 80's, many thought getting high brought them to another level consciously,
I watched families and people I thought was mentors,
Become crack heads, drunks, prostitutes not knowing the difference between b's and Whores,
Ms. Wilson was a beautiful woman, one I aspired to have one day,
Later seeing her begging for 5 dollars,
And what she was willing to do I don't want to say,
I guess I'm still not as spiritual as I need to be,
In my mind, burning down the system and who created it is all I could see,
A good man is mainly all I wanted to be,
But actually, people like the above I have a problem see breathe,
And the drugs dealers who reign in your game,
I see nothing but death, heartache and pain,
If it was legal, I would hunt you down,
I don't even want to hear your excuses because you talk too much,
Teens and children killed by guns and drugs in 2005' would fill 120 public school
classrooms of 25 students each,
So, take your last breath as I end your conversation as your brain I would breach,

They complain how 5-0 comes down on them,

Even when they murder, they complain about who snitched on them,

Ask for a solution from the MF's and you can't get one from them,

It's like they prefer the hell the streets place on them,

Even the funerals...they don't mind burying them,

Although the same ones call the police when they want to be saved by them,

I fight with it spiritually but I would show you no mercy,

And actually, the lack of seeing you would make me happy,

Your mentality is difficult to concede,

Realizing you need not ever breed,

And for the users,

I'll never understand why a sound mind would every place drugs in their body,

Look at the news, the rich, the poor, the dead, who's actually happy?

If this is what you do with your money,

If I was a God I would drop a building on top of thee,

A mind lost, not ever free is no smarter monetarily,

I'm deleting people from my phone damn near weekly,

This is your brains on drugs,

And I'm the skillet,

In your mind you have dreams you'll never fulfill,

Look around you, you're like the hunted wanting to be killed,

From a blood-stained life, cold as hunter's kill,

At least in a volleyball game it's common to spike it,

You're a disgrace to the Gods, you're a slave that actually like it!

I'm going to end this poem with one more line to say,

I should call you Toby because you're damn sure not Kunta Kinte!

Eyes Wide Open

I came, saw, and conquered,
A king feared, hated, loved yet many prefer tortured,
You have been there to mend wounds & wipe the blood from my hands,
Many I've saved yet I only think of the multitudes I couldn't defend,
Plagued with boys who are decadent in the face of men,
82 shot, 14 dead in Chi-Town July 4th weekend,
Women murdering their own children,

Small brains like rats yet rats even thrive to live & succeed,
Hell seems to be unleashed on earth from this breed,
It matters less whether their shooting up a movie theatre, a school like
Columbine or unarmed Marines,
Every day, hard-working people are targeted more so than criminals so
it seems,
Not just by programs that fails repeatedly,
But by others putting up anti-gun signs in league with murderous
echoed screams,
This may be out of line,
But crime doesn't care about a sign!

So, who am I actually defending?
I'm hated by most that should support me even when winning,
Feeling proud of my uniform, ironing, shining my shoes showing the
pride in me,
Realizing I'm going in many days to protect people who hate me!
I hear the echoes of their words & see the looks in their eyes,
Even when I survive, they smile in my face wishing I was the one who
died,
Though I'm hugged & embraced by many who loves me,
Many of them disliked me for being different until I save thee,

I know the difference in love & being fake,
Yet it seems like acting has overshadowed realness as of late,
Like a woman having a child by a man for child support never wanting
a ring,
The cost of living is easier in weaker minds with man less households
so it seems,
This is life absent love,
They lack the wisdom of the older Gods & traditions,
Embracing thugs,
They tell me I'm too disciplined but there's authenticity in what I say,
Only one God,
It's impossible that they pray to the same God that I pray,

As a God,
I would seek them all out & burn them alive,
Just to make an example out of them so the good people could focus
& thrive,
So, out of all of the pain you know I've had that I didn't mention,
Love is gone plagued by this world of hatred & dissension!

Gentle Thoughts

Shhhhh.......... don't say a word,
Share your bad experiences and forget the bad men and what you've heard,
It's only me and you here...my dear, so intricate...so sincere,
See, I don't think I can impress you,

But I'll do my damness not to depress you,
I want to know you,
No movie star,
No centerfold,
No million or billionaire whose heart has grown cold,

Don't care about wrinkles or stretch marks,
They all blend in the dark,
You should know what it feels like just to be hold,
Just like I want you to know what I feel...
When my eyes are closed,

I hope I haven't gotten off the point because sometimes I do,
I'm still discussing how much I want to know you,
I want to feel your heartbeat close to mine,
I'll even gently wipe your lip...when we dine,
I'll rub your shoulders when they're tight,
I'll massage your body...gently or with all my might,

I want you to feel comfortable enough with me to fall asleep when
lying down,
I want you to feel that I will erase your face from having frowns,
I don't want to use you...beastly people do that,
I want to make you feel good...so I can come back,

Share with me your fears,
Your tears,
Even your abuse over the years,
Or…you don't have to share none of it, you see…
Just get rid of it when you're around me,
We owe each other nothing,
Yet I'll help you if you want me to,
Or I'll wait until you open up in time,
Our time is not guaranteed,
Not yours,
Not mine,
Time, which is promised to no one,
But I'll wait, if that's what you want me to do,
Just understand that you have a long-distance friend…
Waiting for you…

Hurt From The Inside Out

Some things you get over in time,
Some things subliminally disturb the nerve that runs down your spine,
Though people tell you to live and let live,
It never heals,
Similar to right before being engaged by an enemy in a rut,
The calm before the storm,
You feel it in your gut,

I have children like many,
I cannot save despite giving it my all on many days,
Many years,
Adolescent and adult failures and being used,
Bring on the fire of my worst fears,
I feel at times that I can mentally move mountains,
Yet fighting trying to save them,
Is like sewing a cuff over and over again that constantly loses the hem,
I can help so many,
But I can't get them to listen,
If they listen responding lies follow,
If you invest in saving them your bank account will be hollow,
Then you find you were never told the truth in the 1st place,
You trained every day but they did not,
Coming in last in every race,
Trying to save your daughter or son,
They return the favor by breaking your ankle every time you run,
Even though the run is not for me,
I've ran to save the resentment of the parent I will never be,
I treat them with tough love,
They treat us as enemies with an unknown form of instabilities,
There's no foundation for this madness,
It's like an evil lacking a God they'll never miss,

A parent who prays nightly for the protection of their family,
A child who listens at any cost to those leaving him lost,
Though left time and time again,
Family is overlooked with those less than friends,
Great mentors they had,
Yet stays at a distance from greater women and men,
It's like a transparent ghost that finds comfort in things that hurt
themselves the most,
And it doesn't make it any better that this happens with parent's coast
to coast,
Like there's no helping the undiagnosed,
When they hate the very notion of the appointment,
Living causing themselves ongoing embarrassment,

I've protected the family from my history of physical injuries in life,
Though none hurts like this,
It's like living lost going on a path,
Slaughtered like the movie Gorillas in the Mist,
Knowing this,
Mentally strong often not taking meds,
This pain cuts deep and cannot be dismissed,
It stays 24 hours,
Like embedded dirt unmoved by a hot shower,
The dirt you bleed trying to remove under your fingernails,
Lacking logic of persons preferring a living hell,
Despite those I will continue to help who listens when the day is done,
There are no tears knowing I can't help my own daughter or son,
My heart will calcify to bone not being returned love in pain,
I will continue to pray for the lives others,
Remain open minded to aid them sisters and brothers,
I have no other words for the good families, fathers and mothers!

I Can't Care For You! The 48th Ronin

I can't care for you,
If you don't want me to,
I can't get close if you push me away,
When you do these things,
I can't see the logic when you want me to stay,

You've been hurt so many ways,
My havoc antiquity is in the stories of my surgical scars,
Yet you were not there for my dark days,
The tender gist of others later identified as spies,
The pitted lies,
Childhood critical care thoughts of suicide,
On occasion when I was the savior,
In aforethought bloodied seen as the monster,
Liberating voices of reason,
Others found unstable like the weather and time changing seasons,
Others switched from friend to treasonous,
Needing a friend though bleeding out internally,
You never saw the pain Dilaudid couldn't remedy,

I guess if on the surface things looks OK,
You will never ask to share my pain,
And fail to realize I need you close as you walk away,
I was told to be openly honest,
Conscientious of always being honest with you,
I was told to share my innermost feelings,
As yet never had the opportunity to,
Because the scars of others,
Made you feel I would leave more scars,
Tears you shared depressed & alone,

Made you feel you could never atone,
Like the image in the mirror left after clearing the steam on the glass,

Low & desolate though I've done nothing to ever hurt you,
The wall in your heart never gave me the opportunity to,
I realize I'm wasting time loving & caring for you,
Though I have a sea of souls & demons,
Even if I loved you,
You compare me to a multitude of people who failed you,

You're alone feeling lost & used from within,
A world of misplaced sins,
Yet you missed knowing my soul as the 48th Ronin!
I will watch & back away like a photo trapped behind the glass of a picture,
Though I could be the foundation to repair your heart,
I will overlook seeing others give you knew sutures!

I Stand

I stood before the worse of society and I still stand,
I stood with fears and tears without help over years but I still stand,
I was weakened on many occasions and wanted to fall,
I felt as though I would be letting down my God even if they stand
before me 8 feet tall,
Beaten like water lands at the end of waterfalls,
I still stand until the day I am called,

My God,
I await the day you make a place for me,
Until then, many stare at me with envy,
I don't understand this hatred, whatever is this thing,
I have little to nothing,
Maybe it's because I don't drink, smoke or do drugs,
Maybe it's because I'm active in my community as block club
chairman and don't like thugs,

Maybe it's because under any conditions I will stand and fight,
Even if they win,
I'll train harder to engage them on another night,
Maybe it's because their gun shots have not killed me,
Maybe it's because although stabbed several times life is still within me,
Maybe it's simply because I will fight ignorance and injustice as long as
I can,
Maybe... I'm just the better man,

I'm no better than those who have stood before me,
I just will not allow them to die without being a part of me,
I will not question what goes on in the afterlife,
God living within me will have to suffice,

My lord,
I will continue to remain strong as only the strong survives,
I will also do my best at staying alive,
Until the day my strength is no more and I one day witness my fate,
When present before them,
I only ask that you open heaven's gates,

I Stand!

I Was Told

I was told to treat others the way you want to be treated,
I later learned many don't like good treatment,
Most scorned with resentment, hating you for what others did, even when loving them,
Their mind burned from those who hurt them,
Scorn themselves sitting & spinning in a brainstorm of illogical facts, so they can't love you back,
Though you've done so much to prove yourself, they only see a future attack,
So, they act hard not showing their soft side, even with their clothes off,
Vulnerable showing their back side,

Things I was told I've found not necessarily true,
I was told to do my best as a child in everything you do,
I was told to hold dear everyone close to you,
Only later in the chaos of minds to find many will hate you,
Though true to whom you are,
It's weird like a person reluctant to see the big dipper in the stars,
Like being withdrawn from believing there's space or a cosmos,
Lack of thought or thoughtless,
You embody the prince song Adore,
They fear being hurt in love so they hurt you more,
Like constantly removing a scab healing on your skin,
Making you vulnerable to hurt and infection again,

I was told to hold the door for a woman,
Never knowing some was as hard as men,
Responses so cold,
Your question is worth your time holding the door again,

I was told what you put out in the universe you will receive,
Yet even as a child my tears calcified due to the many times I grieved,
I was told to stay out of trouble and secure the innocent,
Yet many times I've witnessed the innocent becoming heaven sent,
I was told many things that in another world may be true,
Yet wisdom taught me life is all about what type of man or woman are you,
So don't get caught up in the evil that men do,

Be the voice of reasoning and show the God in you,
And those who want to strip away your spirituality and kindness,
Allow yourself to fall into the darkness embodying vengeance,
Once the threat is eliminated,
Ease your mind clearing it of hatred,
Yet never be the cause of the pain and suffering creating it!
I was told…

Taharka Ankhenaton

If I Didn't Make It Back

It wasn't because I wanted to leave you,
Apparently, something unexpected happened,
So, I will have to miss you,
And you will live on although you would miss me too,

If I didn't make it back,
There were a lot of things I wanted to live on to do,
Hopefully what I've done thus far was enough although it's never enough,
Enough to prepare you without me too,

If I didn't make it back,
I was strong enough to not care if it happened quickly,
Many will probably tell you this,
In reality,
It didn't happen to them so they could not know this,
The fact is that I'm not here anymore,
Share your hugs, love, and memories about me,
For this, I would truly adore,

If I didn't make it back,
To the God's, who would take care of my sons?
My queen is strong she is,
But she relied on me when the day's obstacles were done,
Hopefully, the ora that's within me is within them too,
Strong are they,
So strong they must be,
A warrior lives within them,
So warriors came from me,
You stand despite who wants you to fall,
You shed your tears and your fears later,

When faced with adversity,
You stand 10 feet tall,
In thirst,
With no fountain,
You await the water that falls from the side of the mountain,
When others deceive you and father time tells,
You call upon the Gods when all else fails,
Despite where others failed,
Standing with others or alone,
You pull the sword out the stone,
You can't see your father with you,
In spirit,
I'm standing right beside you,
I'm not talking lowly,
I'm loud,
Telling you to defeat the ones that stand before you,
But be smart my sons,
Don't try to defeat the whole crowd,
My father was not there,
Win or lose,
I will be there,
If life gets to you,
And if you can't defeat the multiple issues around you,
Too many came on too fast,
I will be waiting for you,
Alas,
If I didn't make it back,
Those that know me,
Know I will miss thee,
For those that look forward to my demise,
Say it standing before me,
And prepare to face your enemy!
I'm working on it but sometimes spirituality is what I lack,
I'm working on it like my culture and being proud to be black,

I will work to show it when I return,
In the event I don't make it back!

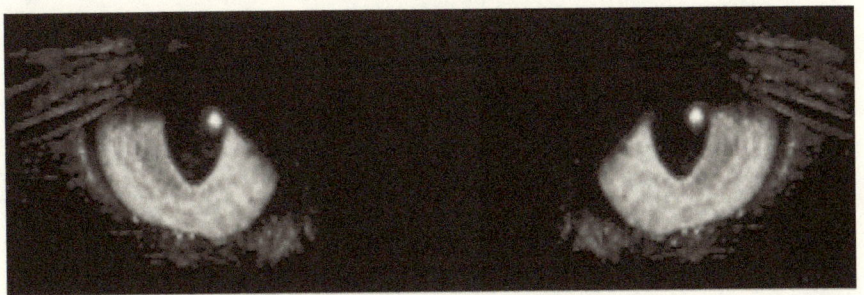

Last Night, I Heard My People Cry

Last night, I had a horrible dream,
It seemed so true so it seemed,
The dream was so deep,
I awakened in sweat from twisting and turning in my sleep,
I watch grown men and little boys fry,
Death row, lethal injections and electric chairs,
I watch people who thought they knew it all die,
I watched tough guys imprisoned in white t-shirts,
Robbing, stealing and selling in the hood,
Later seen having to sit down when they pee and wear skirts,
Didn't they know that many imprisoned will never leave?
Will never touch a woman again,
Only look forward to her bereave,
Why do so many of my people have to die?
Constant anger, envy and lies,
Last night, I heard my people cry!

I dreamt of the River Styx,
Water flowed like a dark red sea,
Thick,
I recognized many ungodly faces,
From different neighborhoods, news and different places,
The scenery was almost dark,
Very dreary, a lot of humidity in the air,
Absent spirituality,
Absent anywhere you would ever want to be,
A child would never vision this as a place to have fun,
It was dreary with a light rain,
The River Styx will never see the sun,
As far as the eyes could see,
One thing was apparent,

No one could leave,
Why so many of my people have to die,
Constant anger, envy and lies,
Last night, I heard my people cry!

I dreamt of the old block,
Drive by shootings,
I saw the holes in their heads from being shot,
I saw entire gangs,
In their cries I heard their pains,
What the hell were they thinking?
This cycle repeated over and over again,
Didn't they look around?
Pay any attention to history repeating itself?
Or continue to hang and listen to their inarticulate friends?
Why so many of my people have to die,
Constant anger, envy and lies,
Last night, I heard my people cry!

I dreamt of little girls,
With no one to help raise them in this world,
They grew mostly on their own,
Mothers working trying to make ends meet,
Or collecting multiple child support,
Jobless making money where they sleep,
Beating her
Absent fathers made bad boys lies,
Her inner spirit grows cold and dies,
All grown up getting whatever she can get,
Dressed naughty,
Treated the same,
When she obtains money,
She considers it "the game",
I see her but can't talk to her,
I want to say to her:

Oh, little girl who never grew up,
It's not a game at all,
Don't listen to those like the above,
They want you to take the same fall,
They failed,
This place called the River Styx is another dimension similar to hell,
There grew a deep fear within me,
A tear fell from my eye,
She can't hear me,
Why so many of my people have to die,
Constant anger, envy and lies,
Last night, I heard my people cry,

I see many of us,
Light and dark skinned, mixed and different shades,
All crying in the River Styx,
A vision I would never forget,
There's land before the water with one way in,
No way out,
Altogether I heard my people cry,
Scream and shout,
Men, women and children voices,
A horrible melody from bad choices,
These people who thought they had it all,
Crying together,
While living made their bed,
No longer able to change to be better people,
Dead,
Last night, I heard my people cry!

My Tears Are My Ink

My tears flow freely but not as liquid from my eyes.
My tears are ink on paper, these lonely words my cries.
This papyrus my tissue catching every word.
Though I never say a thing, my cries are being heard.
My tears are usually black and blue running across this white.
And though it's been a long time, here are my tears as they write.
Can you see them bleeding and running down these lines?
Or do I need to highlight them so you can read the signs?
My tears they flow on paper but I've typed them on a screen.
Displayed bold and big across your monitor, you know what I mean.
When those tears flow heavily, I'm using bold, italic font and a size of
twenty-eight.
But when my tears flow upon paper, they're handwritten very late.
I stay up until sunrise just letting my tears flow freely.
Hoping that when you read them you don't just see my tears, you see me.

Written by Crystal Scott Tha'Poet 02.25.2020 9:37pm

*My response to Crystal Scott's poem,
"The Tears are My Ink"

Warning, Lacking Tolerance

"My Tears, Hear Me Speak!
My tears can't flow, my eyes are dry,
I see many tears at funerals,
The redness in my eyes,
Though nothing falls, yet there's pain,
I want them to flow however nothing comes out,
Am I sane?
I watched caskets leave funeral homes,
Tears dry as stone,
I've watched people pass out,
I've felt their painful moans,
Their yells aloud,
Though my eyes are still dry,
The crowd tears flow,
Unsettlingly,
I ask what's wrong with me?
Yet historically, I cried the cries of rivers and open seas,
Later to shower feeling the sting from my wounded knees,
The answer back in my mind is who would cry for me?
The answer in my mind says how many deaths are casually OK?
They pray a lot but in their home the killers stay,
They feed them,
Clothe them,
Let them eat from their table,
So, my eyes shed not the void I see as unstable,
They're strong as nails,
Yet they allow the worse,

It's like God made them prophets yet they chose to be cursed,
And the women who cater this weakness,
Queens with disembowed minds actions are the worse,
It's like watching life birthed a lazy tomb from their womb,
Allowing them to sleep in & not get up till noon,
I feel like Dr. Watson from the Watchmen morphing myself to the moon,
So, my ears fail to tear seeing them in a pine box,
I feel more sympathy for the rabbit caught by the fox,
The sniper, slowly pressing the trigger on target focusing with his red dot,
The child with a nosebleed thinking it was snot,
The woman who loved, yet was loved not,
More so than the protector of the realm, vile but King he was not,
So, no tears from me,
Rot failing everything you love in your coffin or before being burned in your pine box,
I cry not!"

~ *Written by Taharka Ankhenaton aka WarriorPharaoh,*
This 25th day of February, 2021
from 1:40-1:58 am

Self-control is strength. Calmness is mastery. You have to get to a point where your mood doesn't shift based on the insignificant actions of someon else. Don't allow others to control the direction of your life. Don't allow your emotions to overpower your intelligence.

Remember Me!

Faces come and go,
In summertime it's hard to remember the worse fall of snow,
Flowers grow then they weed away,
You normally don't remember everyone you dated,
You remember the one that stays,
Will they remember me?
No, unfortunately,

Of all my titles,
They'll forget me like American Idols,
Historic Kings and Queens are forgotten until you read the book,
Names to faces escapes you,
Makes you hesitant to approach them when you look,
Will they remember in coldness how I kept them warm?
Will they remember when I was the shelter from the storm?
When darkness was face to face,
Will they remember how I kept them safe?
In hard times and concern,
Will they remember how I looked out for them?
Wanting nothing in return,
Will they remember me?
No, unfortunately,

It's funny how people remember your flaws,
Breaking of jaws,
Noses,
Public appearances when you were embarrassed,
In tough times,
They witnessed you in a hundred altercations making a dark place light,
Then they think you're all washed up the day you lose a fight,

As a people,
Diamonds are forever but we are not,
Make your mark in life respectfully so you're not forgot,
Memories are memories because for a time the thought was lost,
Pictures are taken for this reason,
You remember the ice you fell on... but forget the frost,

Re: My Love by Lady Doc

My love,

You have shown me the light in the darkest hours
You lead me back to who I was.
You gave me the strength to do what must be done.

Your love makes me whole
Your heart makes me happy
Your soul talks to mine like no other

What I've wanted all my life, you are
I'll never have to the words to tell you how much I love you.

I am man,

Showing light in dark hours is what I'm supposed to do,
You direct me out of the darkness to the light like a Queen is supposed to,

I'm a king,
You're a queen,
We're like a seam although seamless,
A speaker, speechless,
An elephant without hunger,
Lightning, without the thunder,
You said I lead you back to who you were,
I spelled it out for you but you read the book,
I hunted and brought home the food but you're the cook,
Absent the mother of the earth,

I don't exist,

Your very heartbeat,
Is a total bliss,
When I feel your heat,
I feel the sun,

So, my love,
I must make you whole so I can lay my head when the day is done,
Happiness was already in your heart,
I was the fire yet you only needed a spark,
Someone you could trust and close your eyes with in the dark,

My soul talks to yours,
Your soul talks to mine,
Like the R-Kelly song...slow wind,

My queen,
You need not find the words to tell me how much you love me,
You said it,
Just prove it!
Many have heard "I love you" before,
How many means it like the energy Prince sung "Adore"!
I can hear him singing in my head so it seems,

Until the next time,
My queen.

You

Author Unknown

We love you in all ways possible.
We endure more that we should from you.
We have your children to give you a feel of pride.
We are the back bone in your stride; believe it or not.
We take your pride and help it grow.
We shed tears, hoping you'll change for the better.

But time after time, our pillows only get wetter.
Why must you hurt us the way you do?
Why must you abuse us to get your point across?
Physically, emotionally and mentally.

Why must you drive us to do the unnecessary?
When all we want to do is give you love.
Why must you teach your sons to love us and leave us?
Why must you bring diseases home to us?
Why must the blame be put on us when that happens?
Why don't you remember you were conceived and birthed by a woman?
Why must we be used at your disposal?
Why must you misuse the body of a woman?
Why must you abuse the sanctuary in which your child is born?
Why do you forget that you have a mother, sister, daughter, niece,
cousin, and aunty?
Those of whom have to deal with other men who do what you do.

Why must you say those 3 sacred words, when there is no meaning?
Why must you say "I do" when you really don't?
Why must we be left alone to suffer heartache and pain when it's all
your fault?

Taharka Ankhenaton

What did we do to deserve the treatment we get from you?
Is it because we are women who care for you, love you, try to protect
you, comfort you,
forgive you, birth you, and raise you?
Is it us, or is it you?!

Response to You

Taharka Ankhenaton

I feel for you,
For you speak of males that never achieved manhood,
Never passed their Rites of Passage,
Boys that never became man,
No good,
Of age,
Living life like actors on stage,
Although I feel for you,
They need to know thy history and know thyself,
For these actions were taught and not new,

Long ago,
Through slavery and invasions,
Men and women were used to breed for years,
This in addition to Willie Lynch,
Even today brings unholy complications,
Ungodly reasons for this plight,
Years of mental, physical and spiritual genocide,
Once Freed,
These males were never taught how to do it right,

Maybe if they know and studied this,
They would not want to be like this,
Wouldn't want to teach this,
For every race is affected by this,
Our Mothers of the Earth often don't know to look for this,
As a result,
Firmly affected by this,

Stalked and hunted by this like coyotes hunt in packs for the
vulnerable prey,
Although they look strong to others,
They're futures are bleak,
Good actors they may be,
But these so-called men are weak,

One would think,
Knowing this or not,
One would not want to travel this path,
Yet in my travels I see not,

Many are loving and caring to their mates,
Then change when they see something they call "Hot",
Something new,
Not for them,
A threat to you,
So, they hurt you,
Misuse and mistreat you,
Many women even decided to be with other women,
To get away from him,
To get away from them,
Trying to find love one way or another,
Tired of being used by their brothers,

It's not me or you,
It's us,
For every time someone's love and heart are hurt,
Other relationships,
Hard is trust,
So, we all suffer,
Like a single mother,
An animal lost from the pact,
A child that needs his father,

Year by year,
More and more laws are imposed on us,
Whole neighborhoods once flourishing has fallen,
Aided by bad relationships,
Mothers not knowing their the Mothers of the Earth,
Boys of age who are not men,
I know it's hard for you,
Not being like them I feel for you,
An end quote,
"It's hard for men to find good men to be brothers too!"

Written by Taharka H. Ankhenaton aka Warrior & WarriorPharaoh.
March 20, 2005, 08:28:59 AM

Sa-tan

I never saw you as I have not seen God,
Yet I have seen evil and good,
People considered evil living under certain conditions,
Misunderstood,
I've witnessed followers on the path of righteousness,
Later swayed to become demons,
Those apparently unholy become holy,

Although I personally wouldn't trust thee,
Sickness may lay dormant,
Some bacteria and infections never leave,
I have watched innocent little children later become beast,
I have watched gallant efforts at peace,
Never cease,
I have watched some of the best of society,
Fall to their feet,

I have watched the nicest of society after being hurt,
Never again speak,
I need not mention the wars you placed your evil spirit in,
I need not mention the souls you've taken from man,
You have seen more evil than I ever will,
And if all or any of what they say about you is true,
You will be party to millions more through miseducation, hate and
orders will be killed,
I'm not saying that I will not be engulfed by your soldiers,
I have been confronted by them on several occasions,
Only to brush the dirt off my shoulders,
So be it,

This conversation is between you and me,

I don't speak for the world,
For I can only be judged for my soul to be free,
I don't bear any disguise,
I'm coming to you clean and intelligently free from lies,
I know you will try to take me down but don't care anymore,
I'm too disgusted by mankind having watched failures from shore to
shore, To me,

I see no difference between beauty and ugly,
Until I get to know them,
I will never trust them,
I've seen beauty that takes away your breath,
Upon knowing them wishing for their death,
I'm speaking for me,
Not friends nor family,
From poverty,
Knowledge of self,
Still searching for wealth,
I beseech you with the life within me till my death,
Despite how you sleekly invite the masses to the unholy,
I will not be moved,
With lies and deceit will not be soothed,
Will not be taken,
Will not be forsaken,
You may move the Rock of Gibraltar,
You may even turn like a vampire bite those at an altar,
I condemn them,
As I condemn you,
Words directly from me to you, you may find odd,
Professionally spoken,
This child of God!

Sleep, The Cousin Of Death

I was told sleep was the cousin of death,
Yet when one you care for,
Sleeps close to you,
I think of it as a Godsend,
Not the end of time,
Even if I close my eyes & never awaken again,
Maybe I'll find that comfort & peace in the end,

Or just maybe,

My heart will stop calcifying,
And I'll live & love again,
Maybe my melanin will activate the nerves on my skin,
Maybe I'll feel again,
Feel those things I've caged,
Maybe they're secured with Mr. Hyde,
Though I must be calm like Dr. Jekyll,

Or will the comfort come by you being by my side,

I feel more of a heartbeat than a cousin of death,
Maybe sleep's cousin too shared a world,
Surrounded by millions yet alone,
As though no one was left...

- Taharka Ankhenaton 4/3/23 @ 10:57 pm

The Pitbull In The Backyard

I'm distant like a lake from afar,
When you have to feel the skin,
Deep underneath you feel the scars,
I'm loved by many,
Not to close to others,
Envied by males,

Adored by mothers,
Over the years I bared many scars,
I'm the Pitbull in the back yard,
Many of you fear & is told to stay away from me,
Don't come back here if you don't know me,
You know of but haven't seen me enraged,

My brethren calm me with peaceful burning sage,
Many like a wild dog prefer me in a cage,
Or six feet deep entombed with my rage,
Over the years I bared many scars,
I'm the Pitbull in the back yard,

I'm not invited many places,
For no reason some hate me,
Yet the masses want my security,
Always controlled & tied up,
I look through the windows at your company,
Good enough to protect you and your family,
Feared by the visitors in the community,
Many prefer to get rid of me,
Wanted when you fear an enemy,
Over the years I bared many scars,
I'm the Pitbull in the back yard,

You want me inside protecting your grounds,

When no one is home,
If the unholy enters in essence,
You value me attacking with extreme prejudice,
You want me to unleash the beast within,
Then you later decide my fate after my sins,

Since you were too weak to do on your own,
And even your strongest,
Would have failed to destroy because their minds can't atone,
Feel for the fallen misery & death,

Empty inside like their soul left,
Over the years I bared many scars,
I'm the Pitbull in the back yard,
I spiritually find my true friends in the backyard with me,
They barely have to come to visit me,
We're busy providing comfort to others on a daily basis,

We live in the backyard,
They live in a peaceful oasis,
Easy brothers & sisters as we know our souls are true,
For all the evil we rid from the earth & will continue to do,

I love you,

For I know you're in your backyards too!
Over the years I bared many scars,
I'm the Pitbull in the back yard!

~ Taharka Ankhenaton, 2/15/2023

Who Am I

I am the manifestation of all it ever was, all it is and all it will ever be,
The original people gave birth to every race,
Though they should be my family,
In turn many hate me,
Not ever wanting to be party to my bloodline when they would not
exist without my history,
Though many failed to tell you, it's your history too!
If you want to be spiritual and not considered evil, tell the truth,
Change your curriculum, rewrite your books,
Or share the information from the books you took,

It's sadly interesting why you would think I trust you,
When you gave me forced religions,
Slavery,
Cut out our tongues,
Raped our women,
Forced us to reproduce for your next generation of slaves,
Beat us to death and hung us with ropes and metal hooks,

Those who denounced you like the Indians went to their graves,
Always telling us not to get mad, accept it the way it is and behave,
You turn your back on the holy yet teach religion,
May I ask?
Who can you save?
Instead of teaching the truth about the omnipotent you make it up,
All these financially benefiting holidays,
People learn their history,
WTF!
Changing African Gods to Athen Gods,
Changing the Metu Neter to Hieroglyphics,

In addition to separating our way of life into dietetics, engineering, astrology and physics,

Many talk about Zion not understanding Orion,
Many fear the year 2012 as a date of destruction,
It's the change of an age, which leads to your lack of astrological mental construction,
You place the man lst when he doesn't exist without woman,
It's a curse,

For inside the womb a child turns in the same direction as the planets around the sun
in the universe,
You lack this like you lack the spirit and truth to tell who was here 1st,
So when you ask, who am I?
Know that I have sorted through your deceptions and found the truth,
I'm past the mindset to allow you to articulate it,
My culture, way of life and spirit,
I don't need your mental fascination about it,
I know it!

~ Taharka Ankhenaton, April 28th, 2009

Witnessed Hollow Expectations

I expect misery,

I expect to see hate with an internal imbalance of chemistry,

I expect to see mates whether bound by love or internal hate,

I expect to see eyes that shows fallen failures of hollowed lost souls too distant to create,

I expect to see groups & organizations out for themselves with empty mission statements,

I expect to see the disunity of couples, families and those that should be brothers leaking on dirt, asphalt or concrete pavements,

I expect failure whether rich or poor,

I expect the news to show the misguided & unspiritual that pride themselves in being players, thugs & whores,

I expect them to be happy multiplying like a bacteria expanding and infesting the body in an open sore,

I expect to see my younger brothers get jumped by their peer group videotaping their physical or mental deaths,

I expect this like the influence of cultural, mental, physical and spiritual genocide that's history was forgotten yet breathes with their every breath,

I expect to see these 300 pounders who found more pleasure in taping it than stopping it,

More concerned about World Staring it than saving the community dying while swimming in the legions of it,

I expect a woman to look me in the eyes deeply and say she love me and would never leave me,

I expect another who shakes my hand and hugs me to welcome her into his arms just to ruin the love we have for each other and penetrate thee,

I expect when she come back to me to say how much she missed me and want me like a shark that loves the open sea,

I expect this like the unheard expectation of a Devil in a flea like a mosquito carrying the West Nile Valley, Malaria or Bird Flu disease,

I expect for others to talk behind my back while their ladies want me to put them on their back,

I expect these things for the manhood they're constantly denied that males lack,

I expect this from people that's psychologically missing sections of their spine,

Like a song offbeat with time and dirty like clothes that fell to the ground off a clothes line,

I expect those I care for to instead of nurture & love me to fail and hate me,

I expect some of those transparent souls to carry the hollow definition of family,

I expect the mentality of my sisters thinking like Hollywood or Atlanta housewives,

Like I expect a wolf to not realize in the meat they're licking sharp knives,

I expect many to like nothing that I've said,

Like I expect you to have smooth skin yet underneath be the Walking Dead!

I expect...

Far From Normal

I never bowed down just because you have more than me,
Logic still respects strong minded people, who make less than me,
I don't love or even like people who mentality is unknown to me,
All I'm expected to do is address you spiritually until known you're unholy,
And I'll never fit in the script of a slave like in the movie Glory,
So don't expect me to fit in the movie Roots, lick or shine your boots,
The expectation will never allow me to share the fruits whether physical, mentally, scientifically or metaphysically,
Not a brother to me only getting close to betray & be my enemy,

And I'm not impressed with the unproven stories you told me,
Or what happened a long, long time ago,
Tell me what good have you've done now or do you even know?
Tell me about your discipline that unifies the people opposing the whore, harlot or hoe,
Tell me how you're refraining from the masses which lead to lonely days,
Instead of me finding out both truth & lies in all your decadent ways,
Words of lyrical tar other accepted by liars,
So much that your teeth & tongue should be removed with rusty pliers,
You talk about manhood you were never taught,
That you fail to find like a good woman,
You're like a person trying to stand with feet that were stolen,
Trying to see absent vision like eyes stitched swollen,
Many will die living the fallacies you told them,

You call yourself a soldier but never served in an infantry,
Start the shooting and run behind me,
You call yourself a man,
Yet nothing in you can define it to be true?

The stomach pains from your mother actually defies you,
Constantly regretting giving birth to you,
You speak for the anger of the thugs & hustlers,
I speak for the anger & degradation of my ancestors,
You're caught up in the Matrix trying to mix & mingle,
Like a person who sleeps with 6 different people claiming to be single,
I'm caught up in the history, metaphysics & sciences trying to free the people,
While you fool the masses in your beliefs like Kris Kringle,

And for those rich conformists thinking you're free trained to be slaves,
Licking shoes & kissing boots is how you learned to behave,
Outside of talking about it, how many people have you saved?
So worthless you wouldn't try to save your child from a tidal wave,
Forgetting all the rich & poor who sacrificed with the blood stained roads they paved,
And no idiot, it wasn't something God gave,
It wasn't something that mysteriously fell from the sky,
That's like looking for sight without opening an eye,
Your history books lied removing thousands that died,
It has nothing to do with character and nothing to do with luck,
That just tells me you're rich & educated, yet stupid as fuck!

Just like you idiots showing off gun shot wounds,
God was behind the science that saved you, yet you deserve a tomb,
They must of forgot the Cat Scan to view your brain,
They would have seen holes hollowly lined with ignorance & pain,
Questionably sane, substandard and inhumane,
Pouring out liquor instead of libation for the slain,
Let's stop giving soft messages that takes away from the truth,
The good, spiritual & sane knows this has nothing to do with you,
And don't ask why the message isn't nice,
It's like accepting to coexist with mice & lice,
Or forgiving the devil that stabbed you in the back with a knife,

Who only talked to you to find out more about your personal life,
You wouldn't ask me to forgive someone who came as an assassin,
And you wouldn't dare ask Hannibal Lector for compassion,
As he remove parts of your body to cook, while you're asking,
I'm a sheep dog simply trying to protect the victims from the wolves
that attack them.

Taharka Ankhenaton
April 9, 2014

Love-less...

She told me she loved me,
But I didn't believe her,
Loved undefined,
May be a head game from the history of others that deceived her,

If mankind failed spiritual prophets,
Why should I trust her loving me?
My hands has been submerged in so much blood,
In another time these men could have been Kings,

Believing in the omnipotent power of Gods,
There was no message to say her behavior was untruthful,
And for years she bared the weight of my sins,
Heavier than the loss of a child,
Attacked by wolves in the wild,

I keep waiting for the day for her to betray me,
As so many has been betrayed,
Even to the day of their funerals,
Their final resting place to be laid,

So please don't detest or hate my hesitations of you loving me,
My life history is filled with the very opposite of this truth,
Oxymoronic like a house fire being put out from water below than
from the roof,

Set your sites on others with no definition to love,
I am oblivious to it,
I am the melanin blackness that engulfed your white dove,
Incapable of believing it,

Unless I personally see it written in the clouds from the heavens above,
Incapable of words of undefined love!

~ Taharka Ankhenaton, 1/7/2018
Your turn Crystal Bugg Crys-Marie Tha'Poet

81

No, No Thank You!

So often I offend you because your heart is not true,
What would you have me to do?
Shall I disguise the seriousness of my face?
Know they don't love me but laugh,
Even though the joke is not funny and they think less of me lacking money,
Should I try to fit in although being around them cause a sick
nauseous feeling in my stomach,
Knowing they won't like me until I change my lion mane to their
zebra stripes,
No, No Thank You!

Should I go to work and fail to tell others the truth, though professional?
Should I sleep with women I don't like just to cater to their egos?
Should I bow down to the hierarchy knowing they're no better than me?
Though I'm stronger, more powerful & better,
Absent money, I can beat them in everything else in the heavens or
hells in sunny or monsoon weather,
To light a fire alone in the woods I am the spark,
And in absolute darkness what moves about unholy fears me in the dark,
In the light, I'm seen as a king,
Where these so-called men are so soft so it seems they resemble the
crouch of females never to be queens,
No, No Thank You!

In fact, I know I'm better than them yet they wear nice suits I don't
like to wear,
They drive cars considered better although they have pricier repairs,
They find their soul in materialistic items to hide their low down dirty
nature,

But would buy diamonds, gold & luxuries to cover up their miseries and lacking decencies avoiding God spiritualties,
They hide behind a skirt acting like Hercules or Themistocles,
Politics they have with boats with no Navy lacking testosterone finding pride on their knees,
Should I get in to fit in where I really don't?
Shall I sell my soul to have more yet I'm happier with less having more than I've ever had truly blessed?
No, No Thank You!

Should I turn my back on the blood of my ancestors in me just to be around others that like being slaves to a system minds not free?
Should I hate lonely days to put up with others chaos and drama?
Should I act like I respect them when they act one way but their character shows they lie even when faced with irrefutable dogmas?
Should I speak with lesser words because I'm too deep?
Should I cater to their hollow egos just to help them sleep?
Should I smile when they approach and call them beautiful with the overbearing stench of too much perfume and make-up?
Knowing their covered skin that can't breathe will lead to scars, bumps and more cover up?
No, No Thank You!

And for those who think I'm too much born in a time of less truth,
You should delete me using these keystrokes as proof,
Males who act like men who can't define it that's overkill trying to replace God with masculinity,
Loud for no reason finding no other way to draw attention with thug insanity,
Pants down talking loud on their phones bowing to ignorance denying the throne,
Making noise and act out making the woman feel bad when they were out disgracing them and blame them for cheating when they come home,
And the women that's no different,

Having children by multiple men to aid in being child support
dependent,
Nowhere near the definition of Goddess as your soul is internally
infected with a multiple thug stench,
The ones that should be called women though defined hate the word Bit..!
You want me to cater to you?
No, I like being the man I am,
No, No Thank You!

*~ Written this 10th Day of February, 2016
by Taharka Ankhenaton aka WarriorPharaoh*

"Remember When You Were Not Good Enough?"

Do you remember when you were not good enough? When they said you are a good person with no car? As a teen never sold drugs, For saying no, many funerals of those living fast, Poor communities brought many scars,

You had to be established although she had nothing, Used by many men acting like she was worth something, You both saw a diamond in her but she chose coal, Coal that ravaged & manipulated her body, Never loving her as she was still young looking old, Then she became cold like the DNA she ingested from hate, Hate that looked just like her, Spiritually cold like the men she dated, Who infected her mind, body & soul, They repeated & reinvented the same broken wheel of old, Tough, Remember when you were not good enough? A lost soul that was a Queen in the rough, Used by others & mentally tormented, Funny now how we were not good enough, Sadly, They lost the once essence of a Queen, Reliving the same story, Remember when you were not good enough?

~ *Taharka Ankhenaton, 12/16/19, 2300 hours*

At your absolute best,
you still won't be good enough
for the wrong person.
At your worst, you'll still be
worth it to the right person.

www.stevemaraboli.com

Wayward Child

Wayward child,
What have I've done to make you hate me so?
Can you tell me, because I truly don't know?

I was there before you were born,
We planned to have you,
I rubbed your mother's stomach and kept her safe the entire nine
months,
It's a small part of what a man is supposed to do,
I made her life pleasant as possible,
I tried to keep her away from stress and strife,
Meanwhile in the background to make her comfortable,
I was working overtime and part time jobs risking my life,
I tried to give her the best husband I could be to her,
And I did not leave,
Despite the offers claiming to be better than her,
We made all the appointments to hear the progress of your growth,
The emotional ultrasounds,
The growth of your mother's stomach and the grumbling sounds,
I recalled her pains and her difficulty sleeping many nights,
I recalled this is what she wanted being better than me in a fight I
could not fight,
I was there during your birth,
I watched you literally come into this world,
I held you that day,
The feelings and emotions expressed I can't formulate words to say,
I was there during many doctor's visits,
Many in which I did not like,
Every poke or stick that brought you tears,
It reminded me of being stabbed with a knife,

Wayward child,

What have I've done to make you hate me so?
Can you tell me, because I truly don't know?

I recalled the many days your mother nurtured you,
It seems like you constantly needed clothes,
The God given breastfeeding I believe contributed to you not having
colic and few colds,
I watched you grow,
I was hard on you,
I tried to do the things for you my father could not do,
You had nice homes,
Your own room,
You had some of the latest & greatest electronics,
What more was I supposed to do?
I remember talking to you early on about principles and warrior codes,
But son, it seemed like you were distant and winter cold,
I remember telling you the do's and don'ts in life so it could be more
pleasant than mine,
It was like you never listened or these conversations were forgotten in
time,
Of all of these things I know I was not perfect,
But your mother filled the gap like a Goddess heaven sent,
She got up every night while I slept,
Went to work tired but pushed through every step,
She smiled & played with you every time I saw you in her arms,
As I left to work feeling I failed her like not setting the home alarm,
I truly was trying to do the best I can,
Though there's no book, did I have the wrong definition to what I
thought was being a man?

Wayward child,
What have I've done to make you hate me so?
Can you tell me, because I truly don't know?

Over the years, there's a lot of hostility in our words,
When I repetitiously say things I know you know better,

I get cold,
I get angry,
I feel you never cared to honor or respect your parents out of all the
things you were told,
The feeling mimics me losing part of my soul,
Though I tried to love and care about you,
I fail to understand how the man in me failed to father his son,
Was it me?
Or, in this entitled mentality of millions of youth transitioning to
adults,
Is it you?

Wayward child,
What have I've done to make you hate me so?
Can you tell me, because I truly don't know?

*~ Written this 27th Day of September, 2016
   by Taharka Ankhenaton aka WarriorPharaoh*

Anywhere but
Home – the motto of
the wayward child

www.realmomlife.com

"We'll Never Be Royals"

A massive history from the beginning of time,
Giving birth to every race,
Every nation,
Though your mind refuse to see it,
A common practice when you never heard of Kemet,
Alkebulan,
Nubia,
Etc,

Before your religious books there was royalty,
Advanced civilizations in science & mathematics,
Instead of higher mindsets many know addicts instead of the Ashanti,
Heroin instead of Hypatia,
Carnage instead of Carthage,
The lesser mind desires instead of the Songhai Empire,
The land of Punt,
The empire of Mali,
If your mind can't conceive your people born prior to Egyptian
Dynasties,
You'll never be Royalty,
Your learned curriculums cut you off from your ancestry,
I think & dream about it frequently,
If you can't conceive these thoughts,
You'll never be Royalty,

My mind takes me to that time when I meditate,
And I rule,
I rule over all forms of government,
Ethical, legal, environmental, cultural decision making,

And I rule, I rule...
Tap into the Alpha waves of your brain & rule with me,
Eliminate those who create toxicity,
Or like any great people who were destroyed,
Removed from history, their arts & sciences to the world,
We'll Never Be Royals!

This poem was inspired by Lorde song Royals.
https://youtu.be/nlcIKh6sBtc ~
Taharka Ankhenaton, 12/22/19 @ 1446 hours

"4 Souls & 7 Seals"

All these years I've been fighting to live,
Yet I've also been the pinnacle of families sorrow,
I extend my hand to bring peace amongst the people,
Yet I'm targeted like the main actor in a horror sequel,
And I can't explain being hated due to the color of my skin,
And I really can't explain being hunted by people in the same skin,
I can't argue that there's racism everywhere I've ever been,
Though it's confusing to see other races love me here and abroad in multiple countries I've been,
Many call me enemy,
Many love me like a brother,
Yet I've destroyed many, even ones who looks like me that were not others,
So how could you love or care for someone who don't know any day could lead to his death?
Nor when someone walks down the street of the same race may take my last breath,
I don't know which racism is worse,
Is it white or black hatred?
The ones that curriculum's failed to teach melanated people was 1st?
Or the people who share the same melanin inbred hatred feeling their cursed,
The ones who envy me every step away I take from chaos and poverty,
Or the ones that want to see my blood flow hating their own bloodlines in racial mutiny,
You saw through my gates, stepped in and pulled me out,
Still wondering what's that about,
You were allowed to pass by my Sphinx and Anubis deciphering the 7 seals proving you're worthy,

Yet it feels like a harsh comedy when it often don't come from those who look like me,

You said it would never be a waste of time, you said it never will,

Yet my history shows me though we passed a 7th, there's an 8th seal,

This seal is not broken by comfort and moving on in peace,

It's the blood flow of my ancestors enraged because within my own we can't find peace,

It has nothing to do with you or the kindness of people who look like you,

It's me, and the darkness in me hating everyone who looks like me who fail to unify with me,

I have some love but the hole in my heart makes it empty,

That often times I'm not seen as a brother until a white man kills me!

Or kills a brother that looks like me,

Or kills a sister that looks like me,

Or kills a child that looks like me,

Or kills the chance for advancement of people that looks like me,

Or kills the chance of the home you deserve because the financing is higher for people that looks like me,

Or kills the chance of getting the same interest rate on everything I can purchase because I look like me,

I can go on and on about the strength and demise of how melanin makes people of color feel,

It's benefits kissed by the sun, and how the unholy ones make us unequal,

You said don't waste my time saying things that I think won't make you stay,

I'm going to say them anyway,

Because though I love my strength, culture and identity,

It feels like within me is not one, but 4 souls within at war tearing me away,

1 is my ancestors, 1 is hate, 1 is love, 1 is called fate,

Together they form a formidable weapon,

They only embody as one within when threatened,

I've been privy to creating many cries,

This seems to be when my calmness is no longer weakness and my strength is recognized,
Even when I've disciplined my life to the path of righteousness,
Any outside threat can lead me astray, or because of color of my skin, take me away!
I understand that every human must taste death,
But damn, am I only human when you see me nationally take my last breath?

Born in Darkness"

I was born in the darkness,
Cried when born irritated by the light,
I love to see they sunrise,
Though I feel better at night,
Even my optometrist said my eyes are sensitive when sunrays are
bright,
Physiologically, I see better,
My senses are keener,
I feel sharper,
Faster,
Yet I was told,
Darkness cannot drive out darkness,
Only light can do that,
Yet I'm embraced by it like fire embrace combustibles,
Or is this a product of my melanin morphed with shades of black,
My brother, God bless his soul,
I loved giving sharing his soul full of darkness,
Different until needed to destroy,
Splitting skulls like hitting a wall in an uncontrollable oceananic rift,
Once seen as evil, I found later my darkest thoughts was a gift,
Add training, tactics, physical abilities, strength & technique,
Later sought to protect the innocent & weak,
Strong in actions & serious in words that I speak,
Sought out by warriors yet talked about behind my back,
All because within me is the essence, dominance & character of what
they lack,
Game of thrones taught to be careful "The night is dark & full of
terrors",
Born from the blackness, surrounded by it, fear is not what I see,
Or is this spiritual recommendation a warning to others?

Because of the depth of darkess in me?

Taharka Ankhenaton 8/6/25 written waiting on a prescription from 2040-2106 hours

Chaos in the Void

Ever tried to solve a problem you couldn't?
Even gave advice to someone that you needed to listen that wouldn't?
Would not accept the best of what you gave,
Yet you knew them from the cradle trying to avoid the grave,
At first it was ego that you didn't need help,
Then you accepted the mental scars after the psychological downfalls like a back with welts,
You feel defeated like every resource you openly asked for help has failed,
You even knew exactly what was needed,
Yet no one heard you like polishing brass with each stroke getting darker feeling defeated,
You knew and heard of so many suicides,
Wish you could have done something and gave them resources before they died,
Then there's the cold, hard truth,
Even when you did reach out to help another, many of your requests were denied,
You're trying to help another with a chemical imbalance guiding them to do right, Truth is,
Watching them fall over and over again keeps you up at night,
You get the late night call they're on suicide watch,
What kind of psychological experts do we rely on in the hospital this time if this is the 10th time?
The calls that they're admitted to the hospital due to self-medicating feeling like time stops,
The disrespect when in crisis,
The outbursts,
Almost losing your job due to domestic violence when you try to help them the most,
Who hears the Chaos in the Void?
Crying out why did you do this or that trying to understand,

You can't as you hear nothing from the voices making them confused and paranoid,
This is them being pulled down the rabbit hole in the void,
Then society blaming you saying you're a terrible mother or father,
Though you spend a decade in the void they didn't spend a day in to understand,
All these prayers still make you feel weak as a woman or man,
Society doesn't know you've done all you can,
How does one keep investing in something with no return?
Even when the expectation is to simply accept recovering ½ in earnings,
Deep loss in your personal state, emotions and feelings,
I can't image what they're going through,
It's like being forced to jump train tracks as they engine you try to avoid,
But it hits you little by little taking pieces of bone and flesh from you,
This is a family member or loved ones Chaos in the Void!

Written this 16th Day of December, 2021
By Taharka Ankhenaton aka WarriorPharaoh

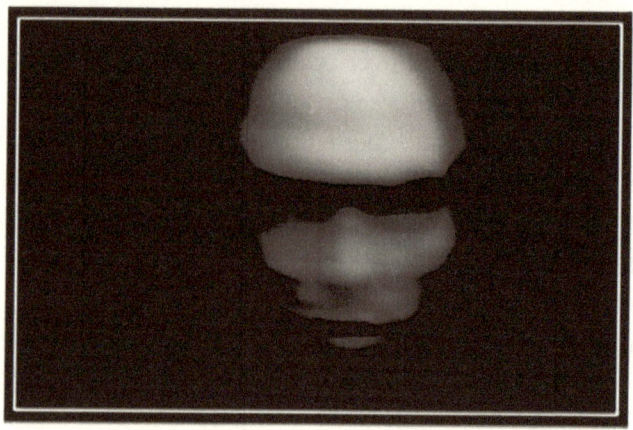

"Thank you for taking the time to read my book. As we all know, time is precious. I can only hope you found value in reading parts of my soul that aided me in focusing through life's multiple storms, the bitter & the sweet seemingly without an umbrella or raincoat. Instead of fighting the storm, embrace it, after all, you're waterproof."

Taharka Ankhenaton